Illustrated by
Colin Mier

CROWN PUBLISHERS INC

MEASURING

Always measure ingredients accurately. In the
United States we measure by volume (that is by
the amount of space that the ingredient takes up)
in a specially marked measuring cup. Volume is
not weight, so although 1 cup flour = 4 oz, 1 cup
sugar (which is heavier) = 8 oz! Most cups are
made of heatproof glass and marked with
ounces (oz), cups and pints (1 pint = 2 cups = 16
oz), and with fractions of cups – ⅓, ½, ⅔, 1 cup
and so on.

For dry ingredients, such as flour or sugar, it is
easier to use measuring cups which come in sets
of four sizes – ¼, ⅓, ½ and 1 cup. Fill the
appropriate cup, look at it at eye level and make
sure the top is flat, smooth off any excess if
necessary.

Remember that where we say *tablespoon* or
teaspoon we are using special measuring
spoons which also come in sets. Do not confuse
these with the spoons you use at the table. They
are *always* measured level, never heaped. The
important thing is to be accurate, so take your time.

This book is for you. We want you to know that cooking can be as much fun as eating. That's why we've chosen your favorite food from your favorite restaurants. We've even asked the chefs there to show you how to make it. But before you start, these are

THE RULES OF THE KITCHEN

Check with your regular chef – in most homes this will be your mother or father – to make sure that you have permission to work in the kitchen.
Chefs are notoriously temperamental.

Wash your hands – gray pastry looks very strange.

Wear an apron or coverall – even great chefs wear aprons.

Get ingredients and utensils together before you start (a hot dog with no "dog" to go in it is a sad sight).

Read right through the recipe and if there is anything you do not understand, ask someone.

Remember, the best chef is a careful chef.

Knives CUT – cut with the knife blade away from you.

Fat SPITS – don't turn up the heat too high.

Boiling water SCALDS – push pan handles to the back of the cooker.

Electricity SHOCKS – don't touch sockets with wet hands.

When in doubt call in your regular chef to assist you.

Clean up when you have finished. That way you will be a welcome cook the next time.

PIZZA

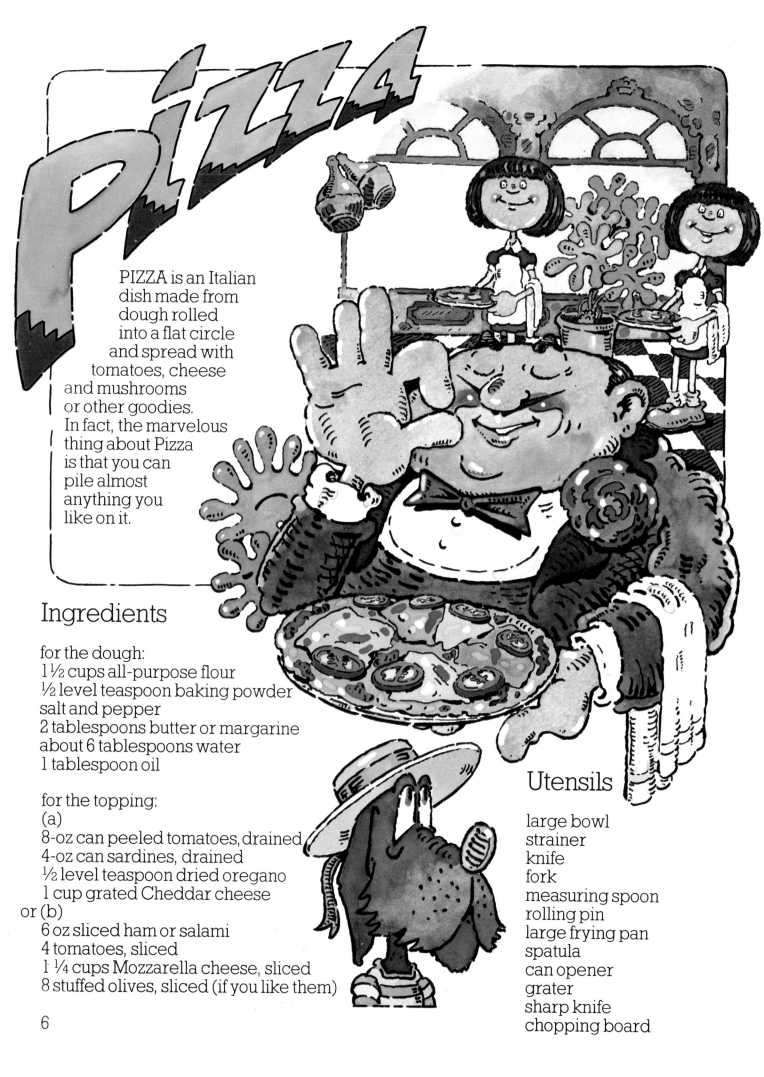

PIZZA is an Italian dish made from dough rolled into a flat circle and spread with tomatoes, cheese and mushrooms or other goodies. In fact, the marvelous thing about Pizza is that you can pile almost anything you like on it.

Ingredients

for the dough:
1 ½ cups all-purpose flour
½ level teaspoon baking powder
salt and pepper
2 tablespoons butter or margarine
about 6 tablespoons water
1 tablespoon oil

for the topping:
(a)
8-oz can peeled tomatoes, drained
4-oz can sardines, drained
½ level teaspoon dried oregano
1 cup grated Cheddar cheese
or (b)
6 oz sliced ham or salami
4 tomatoes, sliced
1 ¼ cups Mozzarella cheese, sliced
8 stuffed olives, sliced (if you like them)

Utensils

large bowl
strainer
knife
fork
measuring spoon
rolling pin
large frying pan
spatula
can opener
grater
sharp knife
chopping board

6

1. Sift the flour, baking powder and a pinch of salt into a bowl. Cut the fat into the flour until the mixture looks like fine breadcrumbs.

2. Add enough water to mix to a soft dough. Knead the dough gently, using the heel of your hand. Roll out on a lightly floured surface to fit a large frying pan about 10 inches across the bottom.

3. Heat the oil in the frying pan and fry the dough for about 5 minutes until golden brown.

4. Turn the dough over and top the cooked side with either:
   (a) tomatoes, sardines, herbs and seasonings. Sprinkle with cheese.

   (b) ham, tomatoes, cheese and olives (if you like them).

5. After about 5 minutes, when the second side is brown, place the Pizza under a hot broiler (take care not to burn the pan handle!) and cook until the cheese melts and bubbles. Serve cut in wedges.

Serves 4

7

MilkShakes

A milkshake is a mixture of milk, ice cream and flavoring. There are many different kinds, we only give a few examples here, but you can invent your own. The easiest way to make them is in an electric blender, if you are allowed to use it. Otherwise, place all the ingredients in a large bowl and beat them to a froth with a wire or rotary beater.

1. In a large mixing bowl, mix the chocolate or cocoa to a smooth paste with the water.

3. Pour the liquid into 4 tall glasses, sprinkle with grated chocolate and serve immediately.

2. Add the milk, oil of peppermint and ice cream and beat until the mixture is foamy.
Alternatively, blend all the ingredients together in an electric blender.

Serves 4

Chocolate Peppermint Shake

Ingredients

4 level tablespoons chocolate powder
3 tablespoons boiling water
3¾ cups chilled milk
a few drops oil of peppermint
4 heapcd tablespoons of
    chocolate ice cream
grated chocolate to serve

Utensils

balloon whisk, rotary or
    electric beater
mixing bowl
measuring cup
tablespoon
4 tall glasses

Variations

Strawberry Cooler

Beat together ½ cup
strawberry yogurt,
1¼ cups chilled milk and
2 heaped tablespoons of
strawberry ice cream until
frothy. Pour into 2 tall glasses,
top each glass with
2 marshmallows and serve
immediately.

Serves 2

Ice cream Soda

Not strictly a milkshake,
though it tastes
just as good.
Put one heaped
tablespoon
of vanilla ice cream
in a tall glass. Pour
over cola or any flavor
soda you like and
serve.

Serves 1

Banana Shake

Swap the chocolate powder,
water, oil of peppermint
and chocolate ice cream
for 6 ripe bananas, mashed
with a fork, and 10 scoops
of vanilla ice cream.

Serves 4

HAMBURGERS

A favorite the world over – serve with a selection of onion, relish (red or green), lettuce and tomato, cheese, sweet or dill pickles, mayonnaise or ketchup. Definitely to be eaten without the aid of knives and forks. Soda is the beverage of choice.

Ingredients

1 medium onion, if liked
4 large lettuce leaves
4 hamburger buns
butter or margarine
1 lb lean ground beef
salt and pepper

Utensils

wooden board
knife
mixing bowl
wooden spoon
pastry brush
spatula

1. Skin and slice the onion, if you are using it.
   Separate the slices out into rings.
Wash the lettuce leaves.
   Split the buns in half and
spread the bottom with
   a little butter or margarine.

2. Put the beef, salt and pepper
   in a large mixing bowl and stir well
with a wooden spoon.

3. Turn the mixture on to a wooden board and shape into 4 flat cakes.

4. Turn on the broiler.
Place the hamburgers on a hot broiler pan and broil for 5 to 6 minutes on each side, using a spatula to turn them, until they are browned all over and well cooked.

5. Use the spatula to put one hamburger inside each bun.
Add a lettuce leaf and some onion rings, if liked.
Put them on 4 plates and serve immediately with a selection of relish or pickles.

Variations

Cheeseburgers

Top the cooked hamburger with a slice of Cheddar or Swiss cheese and leave under the broiler for a further minute or until the cheese has melted.

Baconburgers

Broil 8 slices of bacon at the same time as the hamburgers and use tongs to add 2 of them to the bun with each hamburger.

Serves 4

CRUNCHY COLESLAW SALAD

If you want to, you can add other things to this Dutch salad, so long as they are crunchy. Chopped raw onion or fennel are two possibilities.

Serve it with hot dogs or hamburgers or on its own with cubes of cheese.

Ingredients

About ½ a small head white cabbage
2 celery sticks
1 large carrot
1 eating apple
1 tablespoon lemon juice
3 tablespoons sour cream or yogurt
3 tablespoons mayonnaise
salt and pepper
¼ cup chopped walnuts or peanuts
¼ cup raisins

Utensils

sharp knife
chopping board
vegetable peeler
grater
mixing bowls
tablespoon
serving dish

1. Slice the cabbage into thin shreds.
   Cut the celery into slices.

2. Peel the carrot then grate on the
   coarse side of the grater.
   Place in a large bowl with
   the cabbage and celery.

3. Cut the apple into quarters, remove
   the core, then chop into small pieces.
   Put the chopped apple in a basin,
   add the lemon juice and mix well together.

4. Mix the sour cream
   or yogurt and
   the mayonnaise together
   in another bowl.
   Add salt and pepper then mix
   in the apple and lemon juice.

5. Add the apple mixture, nuts and raisins
   to the cabbage and toss
   together until well mixed.
   Then turn into a serving dish.

Serves 4

BARBECUED BAKED BEANS

Just the food for a cold night, your favorite baked beans and sausages in a spicy sauce.

You can cook them over a barbecue or camp fire as well.

Ingredients

1 medium onion
2 tablespoons vegetable oil
2 large (15-oz) cans baked beans
4 level teaspoons prepared mustard
2 level tablespoons soft brown sugar
3 tablespoons vinegar
½ lb frankfurters
salt and pepper
hot pepper sauce, such as Tabasco

Utensils

chopping board
knife
can opener
saucepan
tablespoon
teaspoon
wooden spoon
4 bowls or plates

14

1. Skin and finely chop the onion.
   Heat the oil in a saucepan
and add the onion.
Fry the onion for 5 minutes,
   stirring occasionally, until soft.

2. Open the baked beans and pour them
   carefully into the saucepan.
Add the mustard, sugar and
   vinegar and stir into the beans
with a wooden spoon until
   the sugar has dissolved.

3. Slice the frankfurters at an
   angle into ¾-inch pieces.
Stir the frankfurters into the bean mixture.
   Heat gently, stirring occasionally,
for about 5 minutes until hot.

4. Add salt, pepper and a very small dash
   of the pepper sauce, as it has a hot spicy flavor.
Serve from the pan on to plates or bowls.

Serves 4

OATMEAL COOKIES

These sweet, crunchy oatmeal cookies are simple to make and popular with the whole family. Good as an after school snack or, come to think of it, as a treat at any time.

Ingredients

½ cup butter or margarine
⅓ cup brown sugar
4 tablespoons light corn syrup
1 cup rolled oats

Utensils

7½-inch square cake pan
saucepan
knife
measuring spoons
wooden spoon

1. Grease the cake pan. Place the butter or margarine, sugar and syrup in a saucepan. Heat gently until melted, stirring with a wooden spoon.

2. Stir in the oats and mix well together.

3. Spoon the mixture into the prepared pan and press down well.

4. Bake in the oven preheated to 350°F for about 20 minutes until golden brown. Leave in the pan for 5 minutes, then cut into slices. Remove from the pan when cool.

Makes 8

KEBABS

Ideal for barbecues, kebabs are pieces of meat threaded on a skewer and cooked over an open fire or under a broiler.

Kebabs come from the Middle East and are often served with boiled rice, salad and pita bread.

By sliding the kebab into a pocket of pita bread you can eat it with your fingers.

2. Divide the sausage halves, bacon rolls, tomatoes, onions and mushrooms equally between the skewers and thread them on.

1. Cut the sausages in half.
   Using the scissors, remove the excess fat from the bacon.
   Cut the rashers in half and then roll each half up.
   Cut the tomatoes in half, tear the lettuce into fine shreds, skin the onions and, if you are using 1 large onion, cut it into 4.

Ingredients

½ lb small sausages
2 bacon slices
2 small tomatoes
4 lettuce leaves
4 very small onions or 1 large onion
8 button mushrooms
vegetable oil
4 pieces pita bread

Utensils

sharp knife
chopping board
scissors
4 skewers
pastry brush
plate

3. Turn on the broiler.
   Brush the kebabs with oil and
broil them gently for 10-15 minutes,
   turning them about 3 times,
until they are golden brown all over.
   When the kebabs are cooked,
put them on a warm plate,
   using a pair of pot holders.
to hold the skewers.

4. Put the pita bread in the broiler
   and cook for 1 minute on both
sides to heat through.
Slit the bread along one side,
   open the pocket and put it on a plate.
Put a little lettuce in each pocket
   and use a fork to slide the food off
the kebab, into the pocket and serve.

Serves 4

BREAD TORTOISES

Bread tortoises are so life-like that you
may not be able to face eating them!

Ingredients

1 level teaspoon sugar
about 1¼ cups warm water
1 level tablespoon dried yeast
3½ cups wholewheat flour
1 level teaspoon salt
2 tablespoons margarine or butter
beaten egg or milk

Utensils

measuring cup
tablespoon
strainer
mixing bowl
wooden spoon
baking sheet
teaspoon
knife
pastry brush

1. In a measuring cup, stir the sugar into
the water until dissolved.
   (Dip your finger in the water to
check that it is warm but not hot.)
   Sprinkle in the yeast.
Leave in a warm place for about
   10 minutes until frothy.

2. Put the flour and salt into a mixing bowl.
   Cut in the butter or margarine with
a knife and add the yeast liquid.
   Mix with a wooden spoon to
make a firm dough.
   Add more water if necessary but
don't make it too sticky.

3. When you have a ball of dough,
   turn it on to a floured work surface
and knead for about 10 minutes
   until it is really elastic and smooth.

4. Grease a baking sheet.
   Take a piece of dough about the size
of an egg and form it into a ball.

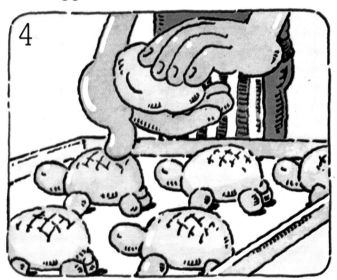

   Place it on the baking sheet.
Add a small piece for the head,
   4 smaller pieces for legs and an
even smaller piece for the tail.
   Press well into position.
Make eyes by using the end of a teaspoon.
   With a sharp knife, make 3 shallow cuts
lengthwise and widthwise to form the
   tortoise's shell markings.
Continue until all the dough has been used.

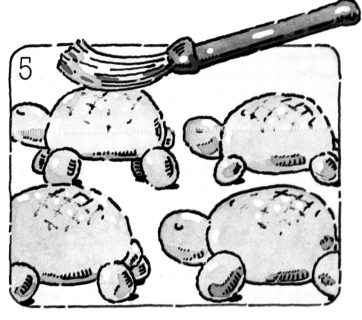

5. Cover with a clean cloth and leave
   to rise in a warm place for about
45 minutes until the dough is double in size.

6. Heat the oven to 450°F.
   Brush the tortoises with beaten egg or milk
and bake in the oven for about 15 minutes
   until they are risen and brown.
Using pot holders, remove from the oven.
   If you tap the bottom of the tortoises
with your knuckles and they sound
   hollow, they are cooked.
Leave to cool on a wire rack.

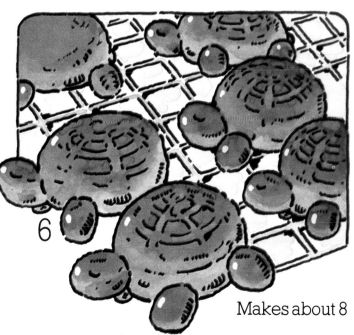

Makes about 8

Ingredients

8 inch round sponge cake (see page 60)
1 picnic-size (10-12-oz) can fruit,
 such as black cherries
1 pint ice cream
3 egg whites
¾ cup superfine sugar

An amazing dessert which is hot and cold at the same time. It is made of sponge cake (you can use the recipe from Chocolate Cake but without the cocoa powder) topped with ice cream and covered with fruit and meringue. Believe it or not, if the oven is hot enough and you have everything ready, the ice cream really doesn't melt.

Utensils

can opener
baking sheet or flat ovenproof dish
aluminum foil
mixing bowl
balloon whisk, rotary or
 electric beater

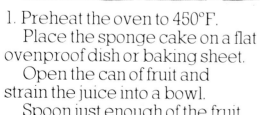

2. Put the ice cream on a sheet of aluminum foil and mold it gently into the shape of the cake (like modeling clay). Cover with the foil and return it to the freezer to harden.

1. Preheat the oven to 450°F.
 Place the sponge cake on a flat ovenproof dish or baking sheet.
 Open the can of fruit and strain the juice into a bowl.
 Spoon just enough of the fruit juice over the sponge to moisten it.

4. Take the ice cream out of the freezer and place it on top of the cake. Spoon over the fruit.

5. Pile the egg white mixture over the cake, covering the cake, ice cream and fruit completely.
Place in the oven immediately and bake for 2-3 minutes, or until the outside of the meringue just begins to brown. Remove from the oven using pot holders and serve at once.

3. Put the egg whites in a very clean mixing bowl and beat until the egg whites are stiff and shiny and stand up in peaks.
Beat in half of the sugar.
Fold in the remaining sugar (don't stir!), using a metal spoon.

Serves 8

23

CHILI con CARNE

This spicy dish comes from Mexico. Add the chili powder carefully – it's very hot! Good on its own or served over rice or with French bread and salad.

Ingredients

1 large onion
1 tablespoon vegetable oil
1 lb ground beef
1 large (14-oz) can peeled tomatoes
2 level tablespoons tomato paste
1 level tablespoon paprika
1 level teaspoon sugar
1 level teaspoon chili powder
1 tablespoon vinegar
salt and pepper
1 large (15-oz) can red kidney beans

Utensils

wooden board
knife
large saucepan
wooden spoon
tablespoon
teaspoon
4 bowls

1. Skin and chop the onion.
   Heat the oil in the saucepan,
   add the onion and fry for
   5 minutes until soft.

2. Add the beef and fry for
   a further 5 minutes,
   stirring occasionally,
   until brown all over.

3. Add the tomatoes
   and their juice,
   the tomato paste, paprika,
   sugar, chili powder,
   vinegar, salt and pepper
   and simmer gently
   for 30 minutes until tender.

4. Open the can of beans and
   drain the juice.
   Add the beans to the
   browned beef,
   cook for a further 10 minutes
   and serve in warm bowls.

   Serves 4

A knickerbocker glory is an amazing mixture of ice cream, Jell-O and fresh or canned fruit, usually topped with a cherry. You can use different fruits and flavors of ice cream if you prefer.

1. Make the gelatin in a saucepan according to the instructions on the package and pour into the dish to cool and set.

2. When the gelatin has set, chop it into small pieces. Roughly chop the fruit.

FUDGE SAUCE

Ingredients
two 1-oz squares semi-sweet chocolate
2 tablespoons butter
¼ cup milk
⅔ cup soft brown sugar
1 tablespoon light corn syrup

Utensils
small heavy-based saucepan
wooden spoon
heatproof pitcher

1. Place all the ingredients in the saucepan. Heat gently, stirring with a wooden spoon, until melted and smooth.

GLORY

Knickerbocker glory is good served with Fudge Sauce or you could make some Fudge Sauce to serve with plain ice cream.

Ingredients

3-oz package raspberry-flavored gelatin
1 large (12-14-oz) can peach slices
1 medium (6-8-oz) can sliced pineapple
1 pint block of ice cream
6 candied cherries

Utensils

small saucepan
glass baking dish
measuring cup
tablespoon
knife
chopping board
6 tall sundae glasses
6 long handled spoons

3. Put some of the chopped peaches and pineapple chunks in the bottom of the glasses.
Cover the fruit with a layer of raspberry gelatin.
Put a scoop of ice cream on top.
Repeat these layers. Put a cherry on top.

2. Bring to a boil and boil steadily for 1 minute, without stirring.
Be careful – it gets very hot.
Pour into a heatproof pitcher and serve hot or cold.

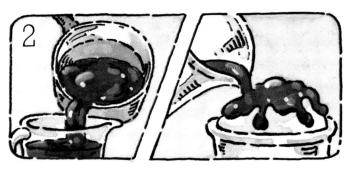

Serves 6

Ingredients

1½ cups all-purpose flour
salt and pepper
3 tablespoons butter or margarine
3 tablespoons lard or shortening
½ lb bacon
3 eggs
½ cup milk
1½ cups grated Swiss cheese

Utensils

strainer
large bowl
fork
knife
measuring cup
rolling pin
8-inch quiche dish
sharp knife
chopping board
frying pan
grater
small bowl

QUICHE LORRAINE

1. Sift the flour and a pinch of salt in a bowl. Cut in the butter or margarine and the lard until the mixture looks like fine breadcrumbs. Add enough cold water, a spoonful at a time, to mix to a firm dough.

2. Roll out the dough on a lightly floured surface to make a circle large enough to line the quiche dish. Carefully lift the dough on to the rolling pin and unroll over the dish.
Press into the sides and roll the rolling pin over the top to remove the excess dough.
Prick the base with a fork.

A 'quiche' is an open pie from France. This one is filled with bacon and eggs and is good hot or cold. You can swap the bacon for a can of tuna fish, or ¼ pound of chopped ham or anything you like.

4. Beat the eggs in a bowl. Stir in the milk and season with salt and pepper.
Pour the mixture into the dish and sprinkle the cheese over the top.

3. Remove excess fat from the bacon, chop the slices and gently cook in a frying pan over a low heat.
When the bacon has 'sweated' some of its fat, remove from the pan and drain on paper towels.
Scatter the bacon over the base of the quiche.

5. Bake in the oven at 425°F for 10 minutes, then reduce the temperature to 375°F and bake for a further 30-35 minutes until firm and golden brown.
Serve hot or cold.

Serves 6

Hot Dogs

If you're really hungry and in a hurry, a hot dog is ideal.
They are easy and quick to prepare and you can make them taste
special by adding different relishes.

Ingredients

8 frankfurters
8 frankfurter rolls
condiments eg tomato ketchup, mustard,
    cucumber relish

Utensils

saucepan
bread knife
bread board
knife

1. Bring a saucepan of water to a boil. Add the frankfurters and simmer for 5 minutes, then drain in a colander over the sink.

2. Slit each roll lengthwise. Spread the rolls thickly with the condiment of your choice.

3. Place a frankfurter in each roll and serve wrapped in a paper napkin.

Serves 4

Variations

1. CHILI DOG
Use leftovers from Chili con Carne (see page 24), warmed up gently in a saucepan, to add extra flavor to your "dog".

2. ONION DOG
Gently fry 1 large onion, thinly sliced, in 1 tablespoon butter and add a little to each roll before you add the sausage.

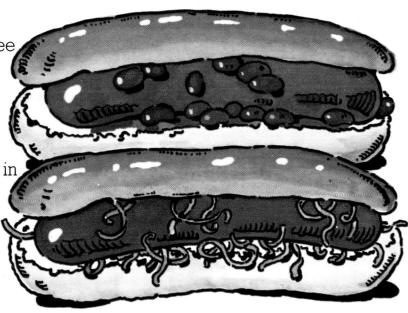

Popcorn Balls

Popping corn is fun. Suddenly small hard dried corn kernels change into enormous quantities of chewy popcorn. You can toss them in salt and melted butter, thread string through them to decorate a Christmas tree or make delicious sweet popcorn balls to eat or give as presents.

Ingredients

2 tablespoons vegetable oil
⅓ cup popping corn
14 regular size marshmallows
1 Mars Bar
2 tablespoons milk

Utensils

large heavy-based saucepan with lid
mixing bowl
scissors
tablespoon
small saucepan
2 wooden spoons
baking sheets
non-stick paper

1. Heat the oil in a large saucepan
   over medium heat. When one popcorn
kernel pops, sprinkle the remaining
   popcorn over the base of the saucepan
to form a single layer.
   Cover tightly with the lid and cook,
shaking the pan gently, until the
   popcorn has stopped popping.
This takes about 4 minutes.
   Turn the popcorn into a large bowl and
remove any unpopped kernels.

2. Cut the marshmallows into
   3 or 4 pieces – wet the scissors
to make this easier.
   Snip the Mars Bar into chunky pieces
and place in a small pan
   with the marshmallows.
Add the milk and cook over a gentle
   heat, stirring all the time, until all the
ingredients have melted.

3. Pour the marshmallow mixture over the
   popcorn, zig-zagging across the bowl.
Toss the popcorn with 2 wooden spoons
   until it is well coated. Work fast as the
marshmallow mixture sets fairly quickly.
   Leave to cool slightly.

4. With dampened hands, shape the
   mixture into about 15 balls.
Place on baking sheets covered with
   non-stick paper and leave to harden.
These popcorn balls do not go
   brittle but remain sticky.

Makes about 15 balls

TOAD in the HOLE

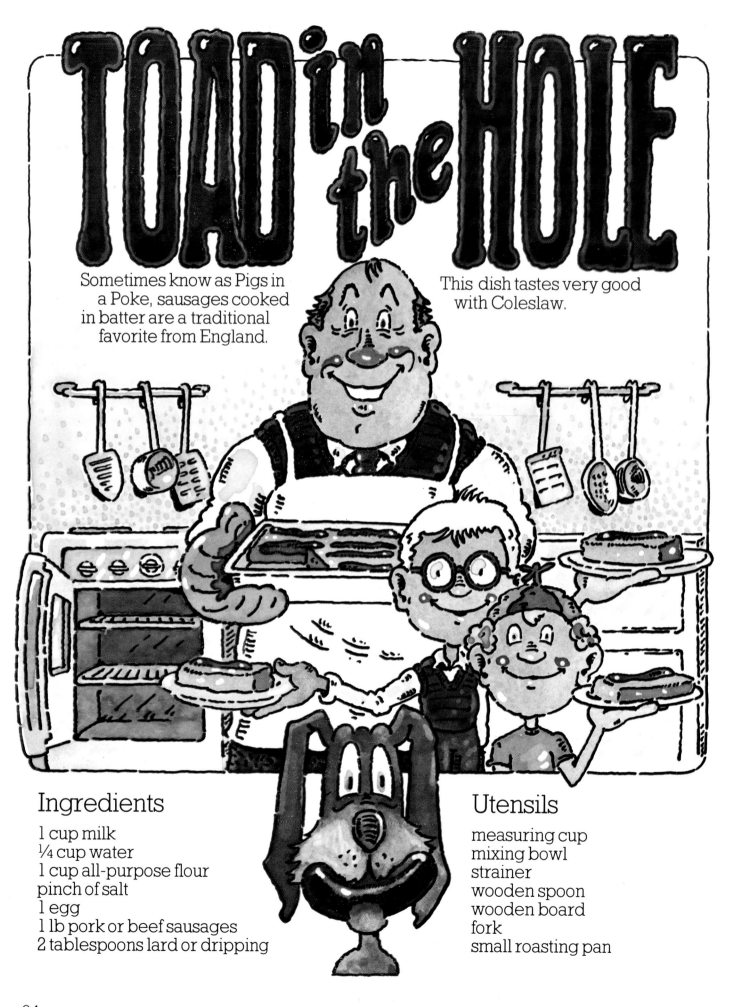

Sometimes know as Pigs in a Poke, sausages cooked in batter are a traditional favorite from England.

This dish tastes very good with Coleslaw.

Ingredients

1 cup milk
¼ cup water
1 cup all-purpose flour
pinch of salt
1 egg
1 lb pork or beef sausages
2 tablespoons lard or dripping

Utensils

measuring cup
mixing bowl
strainer
wooden spoon
wooden board
fork
small roasting pan

1. Preheat the oven to 425°F.
   Mix the milk and water.
Sift the flour and salt into a mixing bowl.
   Make a hollow in the center
and break the egg into it.

2. Gradually mix the flour and egg
   together, using a wooden spoon.
Add the milk and water, a little
   at a time, and beat until the
mixture is smooth.

3. Place the sausages on a board and
   prick them all over with a fork.
Put the fat in the pan and add the sausages.
   Place in the oven for 10 minutes
until the fat is hot.
Using pot holders, carefully
   remove the pan from the oven.

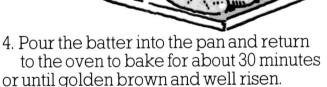

4. Pour the batter into the pan and return
   to the oven to bake for about 30 minutes
or until golden brown and well risen.
   Do not open the door during baking
or the batter might fall.
   Remove from the oven using
pot holders and serve at once.

Serves 4

These traditional cakes are rich, chewy squares of chocolate and nuts. Store them in an airtight container for one to two days before eating and they become soft and moist – if you can resist temptation!

1. Grease the square cake pan.
Break the chocolate into pieces and put in a small heatproof bowl with the butter.
Chop the walnuts and set aside.

2. Stand the bowl over a saucepan of hot water and stir until the chocolate has melted. Remove from the heat.

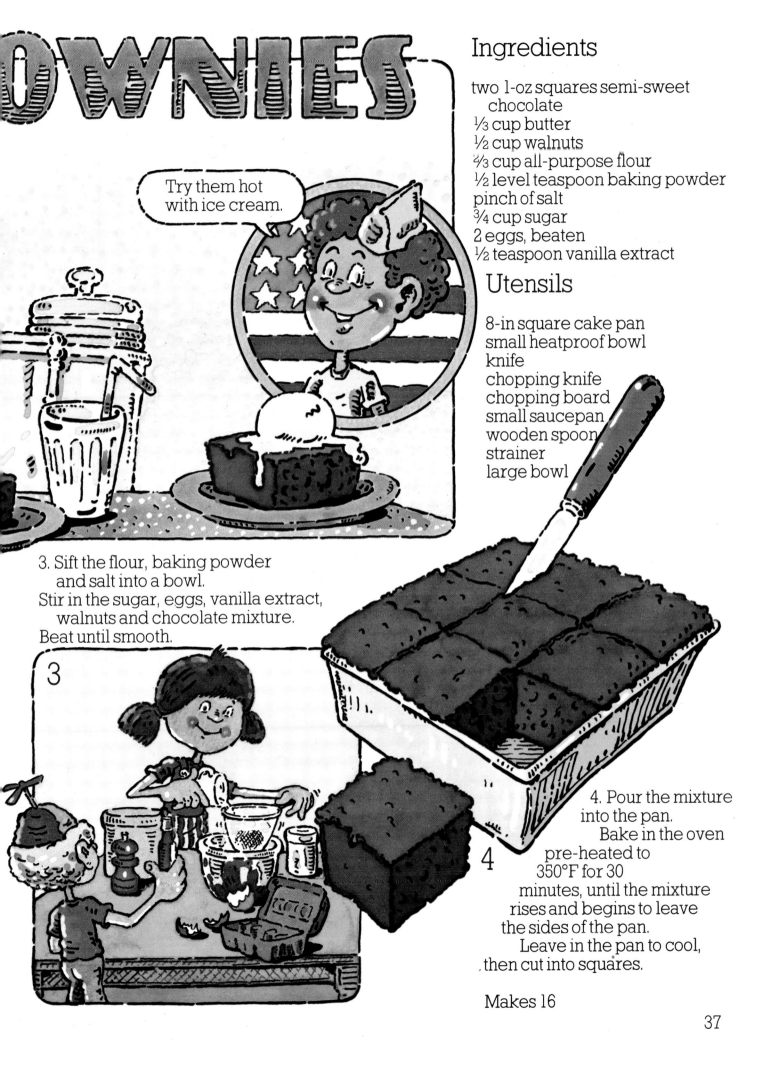

OWNIES

Ingredients

two 1-oz squares semi-sweet
  chocolate
1/3 cup butter
1/2 cup walnuts
2/3 cup all-purpose flour
1/2 level teaspoon baking powder
pinch of salt
3/4 cup sugar
2 eggs, beaten
1/2 teaspoon vanilla extract

Utensils

8-in square cake pan
small heatproof bowl
knife
chopping knife
chopping board
small saucepan
wooden spoon
strainer
large bowl

Try them hot with ice cream.

3. Sift the flour, baking powder
  and salt into a bowl.
Stir in the sugar, eggs, vanilla extract,
  walnuts and chocolate mixture.
Beat until smooth.

4. Pour the mixture
into the pan.
Bake in the oven
pre-heated to
350°F for 30
minutes, until the mixture
rises and begins to leave
the sides of the pan.
Leave in the pan to cool,
then cut into squares.

Makes 16

baked

You can use lots of different things to stuff baked apples. Look at the ideas we give you and then think of some of your own.

1. Wash the apples and remove the cores, using an apple corer.

2. Cut a shallow slit through the skin around the middle of each apple.

Variations

1. Stuff the center of the apples with marmalade instead of the sugar and fruit.

2. Replace the brown sugar with molasses, light corn syrup or honey.

38

apples

Ingredients

4 large cooking apples
¾ cup mixed dried fruit,
    such as raisins, currants and dates
2 level tablespoons brown sugar
butter or margarine

Utensils

apple corer
sharp knife
ovenproof dish
teaspoon
knife

3. Grease the ovenproof dish and
   stand the apples in it.
Fill the holes in the middle
   with the fruit and sugar.
Put about a teaspoon of butter or margarine on top
   of each apple and pour 4 tablespoons
water around them.

4. Bake in the oven at 400° F
   for 45 minutes – 1 hour until just soft.

3. Just before the end of the cooking,
   put a marshmallow on top of each apple
and return the apples to the
   oven to brown the topping.

Serves 4

FRIKADELLER

A favorite children's dish from Denmark, Frikadeller are egg-shaped meatballs made with ground veal. If you can't find ground veal in the supermarket ask a butcher to grind some meat for you. Frikadeller taste particularly good with mashed potatoes.

1

2. Place the ground veal in a mixing bowl. Add the onion, flour, nutmeg, thyme, salt and pepper.
Mix well together with a wooden spoon. Gradually stir in the egg and milk mixture and beat well until the mixture is smooth.

1. Skin and finely chop the onion. Break the egg into a small mixing bowl, add the milk and beat lightly with a fork.

Ingredients

1 small onion
1 egg
1¼ cups milk
1 lb ground veal
1 cup all-purpose flour
½ level teaspoon nutmeg
½ level teaspoon dried thyme
salt and pepper
3 tablespoons vegetable oil

Utensils

wooden board
knife
mixing bowl
fork
strainer
wooden spoon
plate
frying pan
slotted spoon

3. Heat the oil in a frying pan.
   Place large tablespoonsful of
the meat mixture in the pan,
   and fry for 5 minutes on each
side, or until they are brown.
   Remove the cooked Frikadeller
from the pan with a slotted spoon
   and put them on a paper towel
to drain.
   Keep them warm while
you cook the rest of the
   mixture in the same way.

Serves 6

FRENCH

Ingredients

4 slices of day-old white bread
1 egg
2 tablespoons milk
2 tablespoons butter or vegetable oil

Utensils

bread knife
bread board
small bowl
fork
frying pan
spatula

TOAST

Good for breakfast or as a snack. You can serve it with either sugar or maple syrup.

1. Cut the crusts off the bread and then cut the slices in half from corner to corner to make two triangles.

2. Beat the egg in the bowl with a fork and then stir in the milk.

3. Heat the oil in the frying pan or on a griddle. Quickly coat the bread slices on both sides in the egg mixture and then fry for 1-2 minutes until golden brown. Using a spatula, turn the bread over and cook the second side. Remove from the pan and keep warm.

Continue until all the bread has been fried.
Serve hot.

Serves 4

43

GINGERNUT CHEESECAKE

Traditionally a cheesecake is a mixture of cream cheese, eggs and sugar baked in a pie shell. But there are many versions, some of which, like this one, are set with gelatin and chilled in the refrigerator.

1. Put the crackers in a strong plastic bag. Place the bag on a wooden board, hold the open end tightly in one hand and, using a rolling pin in your other hand, crush the crackers finely by gently hitting them with the rolling pin. Place the crumbs in a mixing bowl and stir in the ginger.

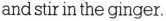

2. Melt the butter or margarine gently in a saucepan. Pour on to the cracker crumbs and mix well with a wooden spoon. Spoon the mixture into the pan and press it well into the base. Place in the refrigerator while you make the filling.

Ingredients

8 oz graham crackers
⅛ level teaspoon ground ginger
½ cup butter or margarine
1 lb cream cheese
¼ cup sugar
½ cup light cream
5 tablespoons lemon juice
2 level teaspoons unflavored gelatin
1 picnic size (11-oz) can mandarin oranges

Utensils

strong plastic bag
rolling pin
2 mixing bowls
teaspoon
wooden spoon
8-inch spring-form cake pan
small heatproof bowl
small saucepan
tablespoon
strainer

3. Put the cheese and sugar in a mixing bowl
   and beat together with a
wooden spoon until smooth.
   Gradually beat in the cream.

4. Put the lemon juice in a heatproof bowl
   and sprinkle in the gelatin.
Set the basin in a saucepan
   of hot water and heat gently,
stirring with a tablespoon,
   until the gelatin has dissolved.
Stir the gelatin liquid into the cheese mixture.
   Mix together with a wooden spoon
until smooth.

6. Before serving, carefully remove
   the cheesecake from the pan.
Open the can of mandarin oranges
   and drain the juice.
Arrange the oranges on top of the cheesecake
   to make the face of a ginger-haired friend.

5. Spread the mixture over the crumb base.
   Chill in the refrigerator for 1 hour.

Serves 10

Spaghetti Bolognese

Spaghetti is a sort of pasta, a flour-based food from Italy where it is made and eaten in vast quantities. Pasta comes in all sorts of shapes – shells, bows, envelopes or string (like spaghetti). It's not easy to eat and tends to dribble down your chin. The best way is to stick your fork in and twist until you have a good mouthful wound around it. Then pop it into your mouth. This needs practice.

Ingredients

1 large onion
1 bacon slice
2 tablespoons vegetable oil
12 oz ground beef
14-oz can peeled tomatoes
2 level tablespoons tomato paste
½ level teaspoon mixed dried herbs
salt and pepper
½ lb spaghetti
grated Parmesan cheese

Utensils

chopping board
sharp knife
scissors
2 large saucepans
wooden spoon
can opener
tablespoon
teaspoon
large strainer or colander
4 warm serving plates

1. Skin and then roughly chop the onion. Using scissors, remove the excess fat from the bacon and chop the slice.

2. Heat the oil in a large saucepan. When hot, add the onion and bacon and cook for 5 minutes until the onion is pale brown. Stir occasionally to prevent sticking. Add the beef and cook for a further 5 minutes, stirring all the time until it is browned.

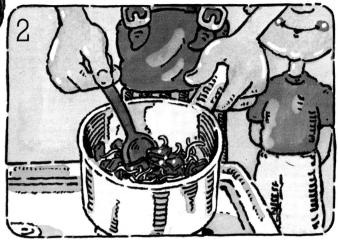

3. Add the tomatoes and their juice, the tomato paste, herbs, salt and pepper. Bring to a boil, then cover the pan, lower the heat and simmer for 30 minutes until tender.

4. Meanwhile, bring a large saucepan of salted water to a boil. Gradually lower the spaghetti into the pan and bring back to a boil. Cook for 10-12 minutes until tender. Overdone spaghetti goes mushy, so test early.

5. Drain the spaghetti into a strainer or a colander, which you have put in the sink, then divide it among the plates. Spoon the Bolognese sauce into the center of the spaghetti and sprinkle a little cheese over each serving.

Serves 4

BAKED POTATOES

You can eat these on their own or, with sausages, as a meal. If you wrap them in aluminum foil, you can cook them in the ashes of a camp fire or bonfire.

2. If you like sausages, after 15 minutes place the sausages in a baking pan and bake them in the oven for 40-45 minutes or until brown.

1. Scrub the potatoes and prick them all over with a fork. Brush the potatoes lightly with oil and place them on a rack in the oven. Bake at 375° F for 1-1½ hours until they feel soft when squeezed (use a pot holder on your hand).

Variations

1. CHEESE IN A POKE
Instead of sausages, sprinkle 1 cup grated Cheddar cheese into the cooked potatoes. Or divide ½ cup sour cream between the potatoes and sprinkle with chopped chives.

Ingredients

4 large potatoes
vegetable oil
4 pork sausages (if you like them)
4 tablespoons butter or margarine
salt and pepper

Utensils

scrubbing brush
fork
pastry brush
baking pan
knife

3. When the potatoes are cooked, remove them from the oven and cut them almost in half lengthwise.

4. Place a lump of butter inside each potato. Sprinkle with salt and pepper and place a sausage, if you cooked them, in the center.

Serves 4

2. PIGS IN A BLANKET

1. Prick 4 sausages with a fork. Remove the excess fat from 4 slices of bacon and wrap a slice around each sausage.
2. Place them in a roasting pan and bake in the oven at 375° F for 40 minutes until golden brown.

CHINESE STIR-FRY

Chinese food is delicious. It usually takes longer to get ready than Western food, but takes very little time to cook. The most popular way of cooking Chinese dishes is by stir-frying. This is done in a *wok* or Chinese, round-bottomed frying-pan, but a large frying-pan or saucepan will do.

Heat the pan, pour in a small amount of oil, and then, when this begins to smoke, add the food. This should be stirred constantly for the few minutes it takes to cook.

1. Place the rice in a strainer and wash under running cold water.
Place in a saucepan and cover it with 2½ cups cold water.
Add 1 level teaspoon salt.
Bring to a boil, stir once then cover with a lid.
Simmer for 15-20 minutes until the grains are fluffy and separate.

2. Meanwhile, cut the meat into small shreds. Wipe the mushrooms and slice thinly. Wash the bean sprouts.

4. Pour in the remaining tablespoon of oil and add the mushrooms, peas and beans. Stir-fry for a further 4 minutes.

5. Add the soy sauce, sugar, salt and pepper. Stir-fry for 1-2 minutes until mixed and heated through. Serve in a warm dish.

AND RICE

Ingredients

1¼ cups rice
salt and pepper
2 cups cooked chicken or pork
1 cup mushrooms
2 tablespoons vegetable oil
1 small box frozen peas
¼ lb bean sprouts
1 tablespoon soy sauce
1 teaspoon sugar

Utensils

strainer
large saucepan
wooden board
knife
large frying-pan, saucepan or wok
wooden spoon
2 serving dishes

In China we eat our food with chopsticks.
This is really very easy to learn and simply needs a little practice.

1. Hold one chopstick between your thumb and first finger, like a pencil. Hold the second chopstick, in the same hand, so that the top end rests at the base of your thumb and the food end is held firmly between your second and third fingers.

3. Heat the pan or wok, add 1 tablespoon oil and when it begins to smoke slightly, add the chicken and stir-fry over a high heat for 3 minutes.

2. To pick up food, use your thumb and first finger to push the top chopstick toward the bottom one. Don't be embarrassed if you drop pieces of food at first – everyone does.

6. Drain the cooked rice and turn into a warm serving dish and serve with the Chinese stir-fry.

Serves 4

PANCAKES

Pancakes were first made in France where they are known by their more correct name of "crêpe", but now nearly every country in the world has its own version. This recipe is for plain crêpes with lemon, but they can also be filled with meat or cheese, for example.

Dress up plain crêpes by filling them with halved fresh strawberries, sliced bananas or ice cream. For a savory filling, choose from cream cheese and chopped celery, grated cheese and relish or cooked meat and mushrooms.

Ingredients

1 cup all-purpose flour
pinch of salt
1 egg
1¼ cups milk
lard or butter for frying
sugar
2 lemons

Utensils

strainer
mixing bowl
measuring cup
wooden spoon
small frying pan
spatula
warm serving plate
piece of aluminum foil
sharp knife

1. Sift the flour and salt into a mixing bowl.
   Make a hollow in the center and
break the egg into it.
   Add half the milk and gradually work in
the flour, beating with a wooden spoon
   until the batter is smooth.
Stir in the remaining milk.

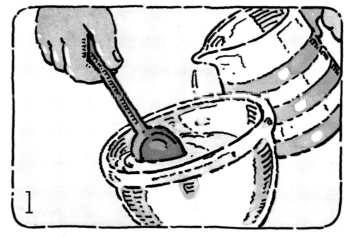

2. Melt 1 teaspoon of butter or lard
   in a frying pan. When the fat is hot,
pour in a thin layer of batter using
   a measuring cup.
Tilt the pan so that the mixture
   covers the base thinly.
Fry for about 2 minutes until set and
   golden brown on one side.
Use a spatula to loosen and
   turn or toss the crêpe over.
Cook on the other side until golden.

3. To "toss" a crêpe, slip it to the edge
   of the pan, hold the handle low down and
quickly flip the crêpe over.
   You do not have to toss it high.

4. Put the crêpe on a warm plate,
   sprinkle with sugar, cover with aluminum
foil and keep warm in the oven while you
   make the rest.
Make more crêpes the same way until
   all the batter has been used up.
When all the crêpes are cooked,
   roll them up one at a time.
Cut each lemon into 4 wedges
   and serve with the crêpes.

Makes 8

SANDWICH MAN

Jumbo Decker Sandwich

Ingredients

2 slices of brown bread
soft butter or margarine
1 tomato
a few lettuce leaves
2 slices Cheddar cheese
1 slice of white bread
2 slices of ham
2 level teaspoons chutney or mayonnaise

Utensils

bread knife
bread board
knife

Relishes

mustard
mayonnaise
dill and sweet pickle

1. Spread the first slice of brown bread with butter or margarine.
Slice the tomato.

2. Place a few lettuce leaves, the cheese and then the tomato on the slice of brown bread.
Place the white slice of bread on top.
Spread the top of the bread with butter or margarine.

3. Put the slice of ham on the buttered white bread and spread the chutney or mayonnaise on top.
Place the last slice of bread on top.
Cut in half to serve.

Serves 1

There was once a man called the Earl of Sandwich who was extremely fond of playing cards for money. In fact he liked gambling so much that instead of stopping to go and eat a proper meal, he had his meat brought to him between two pieces of bread. From this beginning arose the "sandwich" and its many delicious relatives.

Submarine

Ingredients

1 small French loaf
butter or margarine
a few lettuce leaves

Utensils

bread board
bread knife
knife

Fillings

sliced cheese
egg mayonnaise
cream cheese
sliced tomato
sliced cucumber
broiled bacon
sliced ham
sliced bologna or liverwurst
sliced salami

sliced hard-boiled egg
peanut butter
tuna fish
sardines
cooked chicken
sliced banana
watercress

1. Cut the French loaf lengthwise through the middle. Spread the top half with butter or margarine.

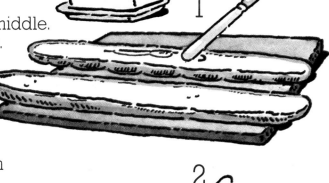

2. Using a spoon or clean hands, hollow out the bottom half of the bread.
(You can grate the breadcrumbs and use them to coat fried fish or chicken.)

3. Place some lettuce leaves in the bottom half. Then add the fillings of your choice.
Add the relishes of your choice and put the top half of the bread on top of the filling.

Serves 1 greedy person.

55

Ingredients

3 cups all-purpose flour
1 level teaspoon baking soda
2 level teaspoons ground ginger
½ cup butter or margarine
1 cup soft brown sugar
4 level tablespoons light corn syrup
1 egg
currants or raisins for decoration

Utensils

2 baking sheets
measuring spoons
mixing bowls
strainer
knife
wooden spoon
fork
rolling pin
gingerbread man cutter
spatula
cooling rack

Gingerbread men, as well as gingerbread hearts, animals and trees, are very popular in Germany where they are called "lebkuchen". The cookies are decorated with frosting and given as presents or hung on Christmas trees.

1. Grease the baking sheets. Sift the flour, baking soda and ginger into a bowl. Cut in the shortening with a clean knife until the mixture looks like fine breadcrumbs. Add the sugar and mix well with a wooden spoon.

2. Put the corn syrup in a warm bowl. Beat in the egg with a fork and stir this mixture into the flour. Mix together to form a soft dough and knead it with your hands until smooth.

3. Roll out the dough on a lightly floured
   surface to ¼-inch thickness using a floured
rolling pin.
   Using the gingerbread man cutter,
cut out the men until all the
   dough has been used.

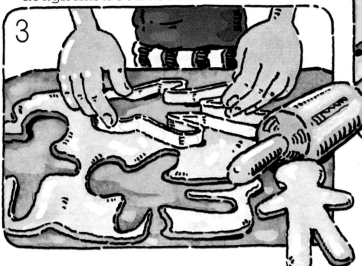

4. Carefully lift the gingerbread
   men on to the baking sheets with a spatula,
keeping them well apart so that
   they have room to spread.
Give each one 2 currants or raisins for eyes
   and 1 for a mouth and 3 for buttons.

5. Bake in the oven pre-heated to 375° F
   for 10 minutes until pale golden brown.
Cool slightly, then carefully use a spatula
   to move them to a wire cooling rack.

Makes about 20

CHRISTMAS TREE COOKIES

Using a Star or Christmas Tree cutter, cut
out the dough. Make a hole in the top of
each cookie with a skewer. This is to tie a
ribbon through so that the cookie can be
hung on the tree. If you like, decorate the
cookies with chopped nuts, currants,
raisins or chopped candied cherries.
Bake in the same way as the Gingerbread
Men. When they are cool, store them in an
airtight container. The cookies can be
hung on the Christmas tree for 2 to 3 days
before they should be eaten. If you wrap
them in tinfoil, they last longer and look
prettier.

If you haven't a Gingerbread Man or Star
cutter you can make a cardboard pattern
for one. Using tracing paper, trace around
the pictures of the Star and Gingerbread
Man on these pages. Transfer the pattern
on to a piece of cardboard and cut out the
shape. Use the cardboard pattern and a
sharp knife to cut out the dough into the
shape you have made.

The British like to think they invented "fish and chips" even though the first shop was run by an Italian in Scotland. But whoever thought of them it was a great idea.

Fish cakes are an even better idea as you can eat the "fish" and the "chips" (French fries) at the same time.

Ingredients

¾ lb potatoes
salt and pepper
½ lb haddock, cod or flounder
2 tablespoons butter
1 tablespoon chopped parsley
flour
1 egg
breadcrumbs
½ cup cooking oil
parsley sprigs

Utensils

vegetable peeler
sharp knife
2 saucepans
strainer
3 plates
mixing bowl
fork or potato masher
tablespoon
large frying pan
spatula
paper towel

1. Wash and peel the potatoes and cut them into even-sized pieces. Place in a saucepan, cover with cold water and add 1 level teaspoon salt.

Put on the lid, bring to a boil, lower the heat and simmer for 15-20 minutes or until the potatoes are soft (test them by sticking a fork in one).

When they are ready, drain the potatoes and place in a mixing bowl.

2. While the potatoes are cooking,
    wash the fish, place it in a second
saucepan and cover it with cold water.
    Put on the lid, bring slowly to a boil,
then turn off the heat and
    leave covered for 10 minutes,
by which time the fish should be cooked.
    Drain the fish well and turn it
on to a plate, skin side up.
    Carefully remove the skin and any
bones and chop the fish roughly.

3. Add the butter to the potatoes and mash
    them with a fork or potato masher
until smooth.
    Add the fish, chopped parsley, salt and
pepper and mix well together.

4. Turn the potato mixture on to a floured
surface and form into a roll with your hands.
Cut into 8 slices and shape into cakes.
    If you like you can shape them like fish.

5. Break the egg on to a plate
    and beat lightly with a fork.
Place the breadcrumbs on another plate.
    Dip the fish cakes in egg
and then in the breadcrumbs.
    Coat well, patting the crumbs into the
surface with your hands.

6. Heat the oil in a large frying pan.
    Add the fish cakes and fry for
about 10 minutes or until golden brown.
    Carefully turn the fish cakes
over using a spatula and
    fry the other side until golden.
When the fish cakes are cooked,
    place them on a paper towel
    to absorb the fat.
Use the parsley sprigs to garnish
    the fish cakes, and if you have made
"fishes" use a small sprig for their eyes.
    Serve hot.

Makes 8

CHOCOLATE CAKE

Chocolate cake always tastes good, but a chocolate hedgehog tastes even better. Ideal for a party, or a present, this chocolate hedgehog cake is quick to make and fun to eat.

Ingredients

for the cake:
1 cup all-purpose flour
2 level teaspoons baking powder
2 level tablespoons unsweetened
    cocoa powder
½ cup softened butter or margarine
½ cup sugar
2 eggs

for the frosting:
½ cup softened butter or margarine
2 cups cocoa powder
1 level tablespoon unsweetened
    confectioners' sugar
¼ cup flaked almonds
a few seedless raisins

Utensils

pencil
8-inch round cake pan
greaseproof or waxed paper
scissors
mixing bowls
wooden spoon
measuring spoons
knife
wire cooling rack
strainer
wooden board
serving plate

1. Preheat the oven to 325°F.
   Take the pencil and draw around the cake pan to make a circle on a piece of greaseproof or waxed paper.
   Cut out the circle.
Grease the pan and use the circle to line the pan. Grease the paper.

2. To make the cake, place the flour,
   baking powder, cocoa powder,
   butter or margarine,
   sugar and eggs in a bowl.
   Beat well with the wooden spoon
   for 2 minutes until light and creamy.
   Spoon the mixture into the cake pan.

3. Bake in the oven for about 25 minutes until
   the cake is well risen and firm to the touch.
   To turn out, run a knife around the edge.
   Place the wire rack over the
   pan and turn both upside down.
   Remove the pan and paper and
   leave the cake to cool.

4. For the frosting, beat the soft butter
   or margarine in a bowl.
   Sift in the confectioners' sugar and
   cocoa powder and beat together until
   they form a creamy frosting.

5. Place the cool cake on the wooden board
   and cut the cake down the middle.
   Place the two halves on a serving plate,
   sticking the pieces together
   with a little of the buttercream,
   to form a "hedgehog" shape.

6. Spread the buttercream frosting over
   the cake to cover it.
   Shape some of it to form a pointed nose.
   Stick the almonds into the frosted
   cake to make prickles.
   Use the raisins to make eyes,
   a nose and two front feet.

Serves 8

HOW TO

GREASE
Put a small piece of butter or margarine on a piece of towel paper and wipe it over the surface of the baking sheet, pan or whatever.

CHOP
To cut food in small pieces, hold a wide-bladed knife firmly at the handle and tip of the blade and cut by moving the knife up and down. Always use a chopping board.

SLICE
To cut into thin round slices, hold the food firmly on a chopping board and, with a long-bladed knife, cut downwards, keeping your fingers well away from the blade.

CREAM
Beat butter or margarine and sugar together until it looks pale and fluffy, like whipped cream. This is usually done in a bowl with the back of a wooden spoon or with a mixer.

FOLD IN
To combine delicate ingredients, like beaten egg whites or cream, with other foods without bursting all the air bubbles. Use a metal spoon to make a cross shape + in the bowl and gently fold one mixture into the other.

TO GRATE
To turn food, such as cheese, lemon rind or chocolate, into small shreds by rubbing it (and not your fingertips) down a special grater. The size of shred gets bigger with the size of the holes you use.

CUT IN
To mix small pieces of fat with flour by using a pastry blender or two knives scissor fashion until it looks like breadcrumbs.

WHISK
To introduce air into egg whites to increase their size, use a wire whisk, or a rotary or electric beater and beat evenly until the egg whites stand up in peaks.

SIFT
To press food through a strainer with the back of a wooden spoon to remove lumps.

KNEAD
To distribute the yeast evenly throughout bread dough. Pull the dough out with one hand and fold it back over itself. Pull and stretch the dough away from you with the heel of the hand. Fold again, turn it around and repeat until smooth.